RACIAL INEQUALITY

ROBIN BAUSER

ROSEN PUBLISHING

Published in 2024 by The Rosen Publishing Group, Inc.
2544 Clinton Street, Buffalo, NY 14224

Copyright © 2024 by The Rosen Publishing Group, Inc.

Portions of this work were originally authored by Tamra Orr and published as *Coping with Racial Inequality*. All new material in this edition was authored by Robin Bauser.

Designer: Rachel Rising
Editor: Corona Brezina

Names: Bauser, Robin.
Title: Racial inequality / Robin Bauser.
Description: New York : Rosen Publishing, 2024. |
Series: Coping | Includes glossary and index.
Identifiers: ISBN 9781499474244 (pbk.) | ISBN 9781499474251
(library bound) | ISBN 9781499474268 (ebook)
Subjects: LCSH: Racism--United States--Juvenile literature. |
Race discrimination--Prevention--Juvenile literature. | Race
discrimination--Psychological aspects--Juvenile literature.
| Anti-racism--United States--Juvenile literature.
Classification: LCC E184.A1 B38 2024 | DDC 305.800973--dc23

Some of the images in this book illustrate individuals who are models. The depictions do not imply actual situations or events.

Manufactured in the United States of America

CPSIA Compliance Information: Batch #CSRYA24. For further information, contact
Rosen Publishing at 1-800-237-9932.

Find us on

CONTENTS

CHAPTER 1

A LONG HISTORY OF INEQUALITY

Racial inequality is a critical issue in American society. Racial inequality is slightly different than racism, although the two issues are closely related. Racial inequality is the disparity in resources, power, and economic opportunities among different races. A person's race can affect the rights, opportunities, and benefits that are available to them. In the past, federal and state laws and policies promoted racial inequality. Today, the legacy of oppression continues to affect members of racial minorities. People who belong to racial minorities are more likely to experience discrimination, but they're less likely to be wealthy, to have good health, or to own their own home.

Coping with the injustice of racial inequality is difficult for teens, especially as they become aware of instances of racism and racial disparities in the world around them. It can be painful to witness some people encountering discrimination and hardship due only to their race. It's much more difficult and damaging to experience firsthand. But there are ways to cope with racial inequality in everyday life, and young people across the world are working to bring about positive change that will address issues such as racial equality.

CONFLICT AND COLONIZATION

When Europeans first began exploring the Americas, they found lands that were home to various indigenous populations. In the conflicts that erupted between these people and European explorers and conquerors, the indigenous people were either killed or mistreated. Many fought back, but they were eventually beaten by the Europeans' superior military might, or by European diseases that ravaged their populations.

Young people today are doing more than merely coping with racial inequality—they are working to fight back against racial oppression.

Beginning in the 15th century, around the same time Europeans first conquered parts of the Americas, Black people from different regions of Africa were captured to be sold and enslaved. Over the next five centuries, millions of Africans were captured. They were put on ships and transported in inhumane conditions to the newly settled American colonies, including modern-day United States, Cuba, Haiti, and Brazil, as well as some European countries.

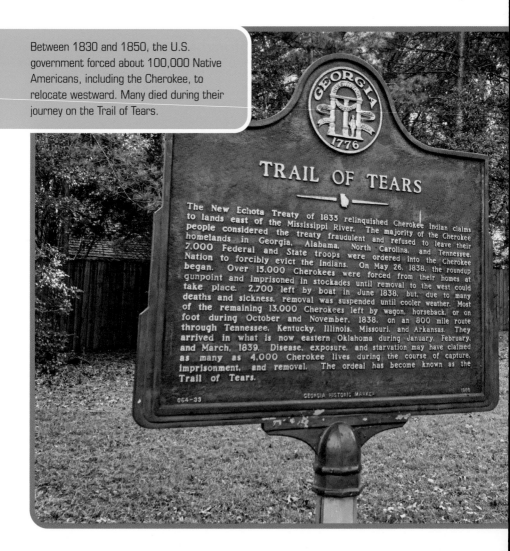

Between 1830 and 1850, the U.S. government forced about 100,000 Native Americans, including the Cherokee, to relocate westward. Many died during their journey on the Trail of Tears.

After establishing the original 13 colonies of the United States during the 17th and 18th centuries, the population of this newly formed country began to push westward. Thousands—likely even millions—of Native Americans became casualties of this expansion. In the 19th century, after a period of conflict, a treaty signed in 1848 between the United States and Mexico (the Treaty of Guadalupe Hidalgo) resulted in Mexico losing all of the territories making up modern-day Arizona, Texas, California, New Mexico, and Colorado, as well as parts of Utah and Nevada. In the century following, both the indigenous peoples of these lands and the Mexican Americans that lived and settled there as immigrants were often disenfranchised, or denied access to jobs and services available to other settlers, and stripped of their civil rights and human dignity.

ENDURING INEQUALITY

The issue of slavery was hotly debated and eventually led to the U.S. Civil War (1861–1865). Abraham Lincoln's Emancipation Proclamation of 1862 declared that, as of January 1, 1863, all enslaved people in the Confederate states "shall be then, thenceforward, and forever free." When it took effect, it applied to 3.1 million of the country's 4 million enslaved people. Despite this step, it was several years before the 13th Amendment ended the institution of slavery.

Racism was entrenched in the United States from the time of the nation's founding in 1776. Even the Constitution stated that enslaved people were only considered three-fifths of a person.

It stated that: "Neither slavery nor involuntary servitude, except as a punishment for crime whereof the party shall have been duly convicted, shall exist within the United States, or any place subject to their jurisdiction."

The amendment was ratified in 1865, the same year the Civil War ended and Lincoln himself was assassinated by a pro-slavery extremist. At last, the institution of slavery was abolished. Sadly, racial inequality was not abolished, and would continue for far longer than most could have guessed.

While the most well-known struggle of the 19th century was African Americans' quest for freedom and equality, other fights continued simultaneously. In 1867, about 2,000 Chinese workers, who had been toiling away building the Central Pacific Railroad, went on strike. They wanted better pay and shorter hours (less than 10 hours a day). In response, the railroad companies cut off their food supplies and threatened the Chinese workers with steep fines—or violence. The strike ended unsuccessfully.

Chinese laborers constructing the Central Pacific Railroad were often paid just half the wages of white workers, and they performed the most difficult and dangerous jobs

In 1882, Congress passed the Chinese Exclusion Act, the first significant federal law in the United States restricting immigration. Even though many Chinese came to the country to work on major construction projects, many Americans resented them. They blamed the Chinese for taking jobs from Americans, since the foreign workers were willing to work for lower wages. A wave of anti-Chinese sentiment gripped Americans—they considered the Chinese "the yellow peril." Chinese immigration was severely restricted by the Chinese Exclusion Act. All Chinese people were forced to carry identification cards. Those already here were not allowed to become citizens. In 1888, the Scott Act was passed, which stated that any Chinese laborers who left the United States for any reason could not return unless they had family here. The Chinese Exclusion Act was not repealed until 1943.

In Montana, in 1876, the Sioux and Cheyenne tribes fought federal troops at the Battle of the Little Bighorn. Known as Custer's Last Stand, this victory by two Native American tribes was temporary. The loss of so many soldiers only made people see Indians as primitive and dangerous, and efforts to exterminate them and steal their land intensified. Less than five years later, these Native Americans were all relocated to live on reservations. Congress did not grant citizenship to Native Americans until 1924, when it passed the Indian Citizenship Act.

In 1910, a number of Mexicans immigrated to the United States to escape the Mexican Revolution. They were not welcomed, and many were subjected to lynching and violence throughout the country. In the

1930s, more than 400,000 people of Mexican descent were deported for fear they would take American jobs.

After the Japanese bombed Pearl Harbor in World War II (December 7, 1941), Japanese Americans found themselves suspected of collaborating with the enemy. By 1942, a number of relocation or internment camps had been established in California, Idaho, Utah, Arizona, Wyoming, Colorado, and Arkansas. More than 120,000 Japanese Americans were taken there forcibly and detained behind chain-link fences covered in barbed wire.

Over 120,000 Japanese-Americans, a majority of whom were U.S. citizens, were taken from their homes and imprisoned in internment camps between 1942 and 1946 during World War II.

EXPANSION OF RIGHTS

In 1868, the 14th Amendment was passed, stating that African Americans were full citizens with equal protection and the right to due process under the law. This essentially meant that they had the same rights to fair and equal treatment in the judicial system as anyone else. Two years later, the 15th Amendment was passed. It gave every male, regardless of race, the right to vote. (Women would not be given this right until 1920 when the 19th Amendment was passed).

While these amendments were certainly steps in the right direction, simply adding them to the Constitution did not change social attitudes about race or give people of color equal access to important resources. For the last 30 years of the 19th century, a number of laws were also put into place to segregate Black and white people on trains and depots, as well as ships and wharves. Soon Black people were not allowed in hotels, restaurants, theaters, barber shops, and other public places. Schools remained completely segregated.

Even though the 15th Amendment made it legal for African Americans to vote, a number of states passed poll tax laws. The poll tax was a fee each person had to pay in order to register to vote. This prevented many poor people from exercising their right to vote. After centuries of slavery and unequal pay, most Black citizens lived in poverty. In addition, many states imposed literacy tests: Each voter had to prove he or she could read, but poll officials usually decided how many questions to ask and if the answers were correct. Many officials picked and chose who had to take these tests, and often worked behind the scenes to make sure non-white voters failed them.

In 1896, in the landmark case of *Plessy v. Ferguson*, the U.S. Supreme Court determined that keeping the races separate was legal as long as the races had "equal accommodations." This was also known as the "separate but equal" doctrine. The case grew out of an 1892 incident when passenger Homer Plessy refused to sit in the Black-only train car in Louisiana.

Segregated facilities for Black people, however, were never equal to those of whites. The decision was overturned in 1954 with *Brown v. Board of Education*. The Supreme Court ruled that segregating the races in public schools was illegal and unconstitutional. In 1957, the first group of African American students, known as the Little Rock Nine, enrolled at Central High School in Little Rock, Arkansas. Despite the Supreme Court's ruling, the students had to be escorted by federal troops to protect them from the mobs protesting their enrollment.

The installation Testament: The Little Rock Nine Monument is the first civil rights monument located on state capitol grounds in a southern U.S. state.

THE CIVIL RIGHTS MOVEMENT

On December 1, 1955, a woman named Rosa Parks sat in one of the front seats of a Montgomery, Alabama, bus. The law stated that if a white person asked for one of those seats, the Black passenger had to move. When a white man asked Parks to give him her seat, she refused. The bus driver demanded that she move, but she still said no. It wasn't because she was tired from work. Later she would write in her autobiography, "No, the only tired I was, was tired of giving in."

She was arrested for not cooperating. Following her arrest, civil rights leader Martin Luther King Jr. organized an official bus boycott throughout Montgomery. As a result, about 99 percent of African Americans in the city did not ride the bus. Carpools were organized. The bus company was soon under financial pressure. On November 13, 1956, the Supreme Court stated that segregated bus seating was unconstitutional. Fifty years later, on December 5, 2005, transit authorities in New York City, Washington, D.C., and other major cities left the seat behind the bus driver empty to honor Rosa Parks and her important act of civil disobedience.

The 1960s were a time of huge change for African Americans and other minorities. In 1960, lunch counter sit-ins began in Greensboro, North Carolina, and spread across the South. The following year, Freedom Rides were launched on Greyhound buses traveling through southern states. A group of 13 African American and white activists left from Washington, D.C., and traveled on buses to integrate bus stations, restrooms, and waiting rooms. As they traveled, other volunteers joined the cause. Some of the riders were beaten and their buses chased and bombed on the road. The National Guard was brought in to restore order.

In August 1963, King, the face of civil rights for many people, gave his famous "I Have a Dream" speech following the March on Washington. A quarter of a million people participated in this march. It was the first of several large but peaceful marches King and his supporters would undertake. The next year, the Civil Rights Act of 1964 was passed, banning discrimination in public places and in employment. This was followed by the Voting Rights Act of 1965 making poll taxes and literacy tests illegal and the Civil Rights Act of 1968 prohibiting discrimination by renters or people selling property. The same year, King was assassinated in Memphis, Tennessee. The nation mourned the loss of this advocate for racial equality.

Rosa Parks—shown being fingerprinted after her arrest in 1955—was an experienced organizer in the civil rights movement even before refusing to give up her bus seat.

A momentous chapter in the civil rights movement closed with King's death, but the United States has not yet achieved true equality of rights and opportunities for all people, regardless of race. The next 50 years saw significant milestones in the struggle for equality, yet inequality remains entrenched in many aspects of the everyday lives of people of color. In 2008, Americans elected Barack Obama, the first Black president, and in 2020, Kamala Harris became the first person of color elected to serve as vice president of the United States. But the Great Recession that lasted from 2007 to 2009 was particularly damaging to the economic prospects of minorities. The COVID-19 pandemic that began in 2020 also saw racial disparities—Black, Hispanic, and other racial and ethnic minorities experienced higher rates of cases and deaths from the virus. Minorities remain at a disadvantage in terms of many factors that affect their quality of life, such as wealth, health care, education, employment, and treatment by the criminal justice system.

Kamala Harris made history by becoming the first woman, the first Black American, and the first South Asian American to become vice president of the United States.

MYTHS & FACTS

MYTH: Legal protections that protect civil rights and combat discrimination are enough to address racial inequality in society.

FACT: Racial inequality is a complex issue that is rooted in laws and policies that denied certain groups equal rights in the past. Many people of color are still affected by this. Bringing about racial equality will require positive commitment from government agencies on all levels as well as from the private sector, nonprofit organizations, and individuals who care about justice.

MYTH: Racism and racial inequality are only a problem in certain regions or cities in the United States.

FACT: Racial disparities exist across the United States. They're present in every state and community, though circumstances are unique in each place. Even if you don't see overt racism around you, there may be racial disparities in areas such as prison populations, wealth distribution, or access to health care.

MYTH: Only white people hold racist and discriminatory attitudes.

FACT: White people may be less aware of racism in everyday life because of white privilege—they do not face the obstacles encountered by members of minority groups. But people from all races can hold racist viewpoints against those who look or act different from themselves. Unconscious bias can also affect how a person treats others from different races and backgrounds.

CHAPTER 2

EVERYDAY INEQUALITY

The United States is a nation of vibrant racial and ethnic diversity. According to the U.S. Census Bureau, the population is about 59 percent white, followed by about 19 percent Hispanic or Latino. About 14 percent of the population is Black, followed by about 6 percent Asian. The remainder identify as American Indian, Alaska Native, Native Hawaiian and other Pacific Islander, or multiracial. The various groups that make up the U.S. population come from many different backgrounds and represent varying perspectives, expertise, and life experiences.

But members of minority groups continue to experience discrimination and inequality in their daily lives. Hispanic people are sometimes criticized for speaking Spanish, or told to go back to their own country. Asian Americans saw an uptick of discrimination and violence after the COVID-19 pandemic began in 2020. Many Black people feel a distrust of the criminal justice system based on their treatment by police and in courts.

These are only a few examples out of many. Some forms of discrimination and bias are more subtle, as well, such as when advertisers target specific racial or ethnic groups, especially for products that are unhealthy or harmful.

Many Hispanic people in the United States say that racism has affected their lives, with some fearing for their personal safety due to discrimination.

INEQUALITY IN THE NEWS

For years, the headlines have been full of stories of police officers, security officers, other members of law enforcement, and other authority figures abusing and even killing young people of color. Many people have been appalled and saddened by what happened to young men like Oscar Grant, Trayvon Martin, and Michael Brown. They also lament cases like that of Sandra Bland, who died in a jail cell under mysterious circumstances after being pulled over for a minor traffic violation. These stories have undermined people's confidence in both police protection and the judicial system. Each day, many are further discouraged by new stories like these.

In 2020, police in Louisville, Kentucky, shot and killed medical worker Breonna Taylor in her own home while executing a "no-knock" warrant in a botched raid.

GEORGE FLOYD AND A RACIAL RECKONING

On May 25, 2020, a Black man named George Floyd died while in police custody in Minneapolis, Minnesota. He allegedly paid for cigarettes using a fake $20 bill, and then was restrained and handcuffed. A white officer, Derek Chauvin, pinned Floyd to the ground with his knee and pressed down with much of his body weight for more than eight minutes. Floyd told them repeated, "I can't breathe" before falling unconscious. When paramedics arrived, he was dead. The events were recorded by bystanders and surveillance cameras.

There had been several other high-profile instances of Black people being killed by police over the previous few years. After videos of Floyd's death were posted online, this latest incident sparked the largest mass demonstrations for racial justice seen in a generation. Protests broke out in Minneapolis on May 26. They spread to many other major cities over the course of the next week. Most of the demonstrations were peaceful, but violence, destruction, and looting did break out in some places. The National Guard was called out in over two dozen states, streets were shut down, and curfews put into place. Internationally, people rallied for racial justice in their own countries.

In 2021, Chauvin pleaded guilty in court and was sentenced to 22.5 years in prison for second-degree murder. A jury later found three other officers at the scene guilty of federal civil rights violations.

In October 2015, Deputy Ben Fields was called to Robert Long's math class at Spring Valley High School in South Carolina. A young Black teenage student had violated the rules, using a cell phone in class. She refused to hand over her phone to the teacher, or to get out of her seat and go to the principal's office when told. In response, the 34-year-old white deputy (also the school's football coach), grabbed the student by her neck, flipped her backward, dragged her across the floor, and finally handcuffed her.

This incident was caught on multiple cell phones and circulated among news outlets and social media. Fields was fired by the sheriff's department. The FBI and Justice Department were also called in. Ultimately, no charges were filed against Fields, as prosecutors declared "no probable cause" to charge the former deputy.

In March 2016, San Antonio sixth grader Janissa Valdez was angry with another student. The two met outside Rhodes Middle School to talk. Other students gathered around to see if the two would start to fight. Officer Joshua Kehm, the school's 27-year-old white police officer, approached too. He misunderstood what he saw, believing that Valdez was going to initiate a fight. He grabbed the 12-year-old girl and slammed her into the brick pavement.

Valdez was handcuffed, pulled to her feet, and taken away, but not before the entire incident was recorded. It did not take long for it to be released on YouTube and other social media. That was when school officials found out about the incident. A formal investigation by both the district police and the school administration was started immediately. Opinions about how the situation was handled differed within the community. Some supported Officer Kehm's actions. Most people did not, however, especially as the officer's report on the incident was delayed and inaccurate.

Because of this unwarranted use of force and his failure to report it to the district, Officer Kehm was given the opportunity either to resign or be fired. He refused to resign, so he was terminated by the school district.

INEQUALITY IN THE CLASSROOM

The stories don't end there. Across the country, in schools, workplaces, and other public places, people of all ages are suffering from some type of discrimination and mistreatment. It starts very early, with some reports stating that children of color in pre-kindergarten, only four or five years old, are already being treated unequally.

According to the Education Trust findings from 2020, Black and Hispanic students are given less access to advanced coursework. In elementary school, Black students only made up 9 percent of the enrollment in gifted and talented programs, and Hispanic students 18 percent, even though they made up 16 percent and 28 percent of school enrollment respectively. In high school, Black students made up only 9 percent of students enrolled in a least one AP course, and Hispanic students 21 percent, though 15 percent of high schoolers are Black and nearly 25 percent Hispanic. A 2022 report from the Learning Policy Institute showed that Black students were much more likely to be suspended from school than other groups.

Alternatives to suspensions and expulsions include social and emotional learning (SEL) programs, in which students work on skills such as self-management, self-awareness, social awareness, relationship skills, and responsible decision-making.

Being suspended from school, especially more than once, is connected to future problems like dropping out of school, having encounters with the juvenile justice system, and higher risks of low-wage work and unemployment. Suspensions are also ineffective in addressing underlying causes of rebellious behavior or in teaching more appropriate means of conflict resolution.

INJUSTICE IN THE CRIMINAL JUSTICE SYSTEM

Outside of school, racial conflicts and inequality are still huge problems. A 2020 study by New York University researchers found that Black drivers were 20 percent more likely to be pulled over than white drivers. They're also 1.5 to 2 percent more likely to be searched than white drivers. The researchers also found that Black drivers were more likely to be stopped in daylight rather than at night when officers would be unable to discern their race. A 2019 study done at Stanford University also found that Black and Hispanic drivers were more likely to be stopped and searched without good evidence.

More people of color are getting in trouble in school and behind the wheel. How does this play out in the judicial and penal systems? According to the U.S. Department of Justice, about 5.5 million Americans were under correctional supervision in 2020. About 1.69 million were incarcerated in prison or local jails. About 3.89 million were under community supervision, either probation or parole.

A 2021 report by The Sentencing Project found that Black Americans are incarcerated in state prisons at almost five times the rate of white Americans, and Hispanic Americans at 1.3 times the rate of white Americans. On average, 1,240 Black Americans are incarcerated in state prisons per 100,000 residents, while 349 Hispanic Americans and 261 white Americans are incarcerated per 100,000 residents. According to Federal Bureau of Prison statistics from 2022, 38.4 percent of inmates are Black, although Black people only make up about 14 percent of the population of the United States.

Overall, the incarceration rate in the United States is the highest in the world. A 2021 Pew Research Center study found that the United States incarcerates 639 people per 100,000 people. Rates in Western Europe, for example, are a fraction of that amount. England has 131 inmates per 100,000 people, while the rates for France and Germany are just 93 and 69 inmates, respectively, per 100,000 people.

The reasons that so many people of color are arrested and jailed are debated and studied by a wide variety of organizations. Not all the reasons are directly tied to ethnicity and racism, but aspects of those seem to filter in even where they ideally should not. In the report, "Black Lives Matter: Eliminating Racial Inequity in the Criminal Justice System," author Nazgol Ghandnoosh, Ph.D., writes that he believes the differences in how the races are treated boils down to four issues: justice policies, implicit bias, inadequate funding of certain programs, and a failure to address underlying causes of crime.

Many justice policies that were designed to be race-neutral collide with the socioeconomic reality. Police policies created to address populations with high crime rates are disproportionately going to affect people of color. For example, drug-free school zone laws require stronger sentences for people caught selling drugs near school zones. In the majority of cities, schools are located in densely populated areas, and have a much higher percentage of POC (people of color).

Many people, including criminal justice professionals (police, prosecutors, judges, and courtroom work groups), are influenced by implicit racial bias. This type of bias is defined as unintentional and unconscious bias that affects a person's decisions and behaviors.

Key portions of the criminal justice system do not have the funding they need, which negatively impacts low-income defendants, many of whom are POC. For instance, most states do not allocate enough money to their indigent defense programs. These are the systems that are supposed to provide attorneys to criminal defendants who cannot otherwise afford them. Public defenders tend to be overwhelmed with high caseloads, plus some may have limited experience in the courtroom.

The country's criminal justice system is primarily designed to react to crime rather than prevent it. This means it does not remedy the underlying causes. For those POC who try to reenter a community after serving time, life can be extremely difficult. It is hard to get hired with a prison record, and in many states, anyone convicted of a drug felony is not allowed to receive federal cash assistance, subsidized housing, or food stamps.

Race relations remain troubled, while racial inequality persists. How much improvement has been made and how much change is still needed depends on who you ask. In a Pew Research Center survey done in 2019, 84 percent of Black people stated that racial discrimination was a significant obstacle to them getting ahead. Only 54 percent of white people felt that way while 78 percent of Black people believed that the nation hasn't gone far enough in achieving equal rights. Only 37 percent of white people felt that way.

When Barack Obama was elected as president in 2008, many Americans hoped this would mean advancements in racial equality. As he stated in his "A More Perfect Union" speech in Philadelphia, Pennsylvania, on March 18, 2008, "This union may never be perfect, but generation after generation has shown that it can always be perfected. And today, whenever I find myself feeling doubtful or cynical about this possibility, what gives me the most hope is the next generation—the young people whose attitudes and beliefs and openness to change have already made history in this election."

In his "A More Perfect Union" speech, Barack Obama, then a presidential candidate on the campaign trail, talked about the issue of race and his optimism that racial divisions could be resolved.

Race continues to be a fraught and relevant issue in the United States today. Despite much progress, members of minority groups still don't feel that they receive equal treatment from society and the law. Data and statistics on issues ranging from hate crime numbers to disparities in earnings confirm that a person's race is indeed a factor that affects many aspects of their life.

Asian Americans have long been the victims of discrimination, hate crimes, and racial harassment, and racist incidents against Asian Americans became more common after the start of the COVID-19 pandemic.

CHAPTER 3

THE TOXICITY OF RACIAL INEQUALITY

There's a saying that "representation matters." It means that it's important to see people of all different races, ethnicities, and genders in a variety of contexts. The issue of representation is most often discussed in relation to media such as TV, movies, and online content. TV shows and movies with a diverse cast of realistic characters help promote acceptance among viewers and dispel stereotypes. Young people from minority groups, in particular, can draw a sense of validation by seeing people who look like them depicted in popular culture. But representation is important in many settings beyond entertainment. When there is diversity in areas such as science, technology, literature, the arts, and leadership positions in government, it shows young people and the general public alike that people from all different races and backgrounds can accomplish great things in a wide variety of fields.

One of the most visible and diverse areas that most Americans encounter in their everyday lives is sports. There's a long tradition of athletes breaking racial barriers through their achievements in sports. People remember the track and field star Jesse

Owens and baseball player Jackie Robinson both for their athletic accomplishments as well as their roles in overturning assumptions about race. Many athletes of color have used their public platforms to spotlight issues that are important to them. In recent years, tennis player Serena Williams has addressed the unique challenges faced by female athletes. Gymnast Simone Biles has spoken about her mental health struggles.

Despite her renown as an athlete, Serena Williams has experienced sexism and racial discrimination on the court and off, such as in the health care system.

TAKING THE KNEE

Football player Colin Kaepernick used his high-profile position to bring widespread attention to the issue of racial oppression. The San Francisco 49ers' quarterback started in 2016 by sitting during the national anthem in preseason games, and quickly was both praised and criticized for his actions. "I am not going to stand up to show pride in a flag for a country that oppresses Black people and people of color," he stated to the National Football League (NFL). "To me, this is bigger than football and it would be selfish on my part to look the other way."

Although he achieved fame playing professional football, Colin Kaepernick is today recognized as a civil rights activist dedicated to fighting racial oppression.

Many people called him unpatriotic, but he quickly denied that motive. He met with Nate Boyer, former Green Beret and Seattle Seahawks player. According to ESPN, the first thing Kaepernick said was, "I want you to know, first and foremost, I really do respect the heck out of the military, and I really want to thank you for your service." The 49ers' quarterback wanted to keep pushing his message, but not show any disrespect to others. Sitting was seen as rude, but bowing his head did not seem like a strong enough message. Fellow team member Eric Reid suggested that Kaepernick kneel on one knee.

Since Kaepernick decided to kneel during "The Star Spangled Banner," many professional sports players have done the same. Others have joined hands, linked arms, or raised fists to display their feelings. Players from more than a dozen NFL teams participated, as well as WNBA (Women's National Basketball Association) players, soccer players, tennis players, and swimmers. Even some of the national anthem singers performed on one knee.

Members of professional sports teams are not the only ones deciding to kneel. Athletes in colleges, high schools, and youth leagues have also chosen to kneel during the song. While many applaud this nonviolent method of protesting, others are incensed by it. Students and coaches are kneeling, and so are cheerleaders, and pep band members.

While Kaepernick did not expect such a response to his actions, he is pleased to see how it has spread. As he told the NFL, "This stand wasn't for me. This is because I'm seeing things happen to people that don't have a voice, people that don't have a platform to talk and have their voices heard, and effect change. So I'm in the position where I can do that and I'm going to do that for people that can't . . . It's something that can unify this team. It's something that can unify this country. If we have these real conversations that are uncomfortable for a lot of people. If we have these conversations, there's a better understanding of where both sides are coming from."

The death of George Floyd sparked massive protests calling for racial justice and an end to police brutality. This photo shows a protest sign from a march in Miami, Florida, on June 6, 2020.

University of Michigan linebacker Mike McCray posted on Twitter what so many were thinking: "Kaepernick has given so many people a voice and courage to stand up for what we believe is right, just like the people who came before us and sacrificed so much for our freedom and for us to have a voice today."

DAMAGE DONE BY INEQUALITY

Racial inequality causes unhappiness and anger, and it can also damage a person's physical and mental health. According to a number of studies, Black people who experience racial stress as teens

are far more likely to develop chronic diseases in adulthood, including high blood pressure, higher body mass index (BMI), and higher levels of stress hormones. It does not take obvious discrimination to cause these health issues either. Just fearing that discrimination will happen is enough to trigger a rise in blood pressure, and cause your body to experience stress.

Exposure to ongoing anxiety, such as racial bias, can even change the structure of the brain, according to a recent study published in *Molecular Psychiatry*. Chronic stress increases the growth of some brain cells and inhibits the development of others. Experts believe this can result in long-term and possibly even permanent changes to the brain in the areas of learning and memory.

COVID-19 AND ANTI-ASIAN RACISM

In early 2020, the COVID-19 pandemic began to spread across the world after originating in China. As restrictions such as lockdowns and limits on gatherings were put into place, anti-Asian bias and incidents increased. In March of 2020, President Donald Trump referred to COVID-19 as "the Chinese virus." During the next week, anti-Asian hashtags on social media rose steeply.

The anti-Asian sentiment affected people's actions offline, as well. FBI (Federal Bureau of Investigation) statistics showed a 77 percent increase in anti-Asian hate crimes from 2019 to 2020. The coalition Stop AAPI Hate reported more than 9,000 incidents of discrimination between March 2020 and June 2021. The most frequent type of incident was verbal harassment. Most incidents occurred in public places, and women were victims more often than men. Asian Americans also reported shunning, physical assault, civil rights violations, and online harassment. Kids experienced more bullying in school. About 57 percent of Asian Americans reported that they sometimes felt unsafe in public places because of anti-Asian racism.

In March of 2021, a gunman killed 8 people, mostly Asian women, in several spas near Atlanta, Georgia. The crime put a national spotlight on the rise in hate crimes against Asian Americans. In 2021, Congress passed the COVID-19 Hate Crimes Act, and it was signed into law in May by President Joe Biden. The legislation included measures intended to address hate crimes more effectively with an emphasis on the increase in anti-Asian violence.

Senator Mazie Hirono, who introduced the COVID-19 Hate Crimes Act in the U.S. Senate, speaks about the proposed legislation at an April 13, 2021, press conference.

Dealing with discrimination stresses the body, causing issues such as inflammation, high blood pressure, and increased heart rate. People who experience discrimination are more likely to be anxious or depressed. A 2021 study by UCLA found that young adults between 18 and 28 years old who reported frequent discrimination were 25 percent more likely to develop a mental illness. People reporting any amount of discrimination were 26 percent more likely to have overall poor health. The young adults in the study who experienced the greatest amount of discrimination were at the greatest risk of mental illness, drug use, and poor health.

Racial biases in the health care system can also impact a person of color's health. One factor is the implicit biases of health care providers— the unconscious preconceptions that influence how they treat patients. Some doctors are more likely to diagnose and treat serious pain in white patients than Black patients. This may come from a myth that Black people are less sensitive to pain, or from the stereotype that Black patients are more likely to be "drug seeking." Doctors may not refer Black patients for procedures such as a transplant or some heart treatments, sometimes because they don't believe that patients will take proper care of themselves after the surgery. When patients from minority groups feel like they've been discriminated against by a doctor, they're less likely to trust the health care system during future visits.

There are many other sources of disparities in health care. Many racial minorities have a lower life expectancy than the national average, with Black people having a life expectancy four years lower than white people. People from racial minorities are more likely to suffer from a variety of medical conditions. Black people, for example, have higher rates of hypertension and of complications from diabetes. The infant mortality rate is higher for Black mothers than white mothers, and Black women are more likely to die of causes related to pregnancy than white women. Members of some racial minorities were more likely to be affected by COVID-19, yet they were less likely to be vaccinated. Past studies have also found that people of color were less likely to receive the flu vaccine.

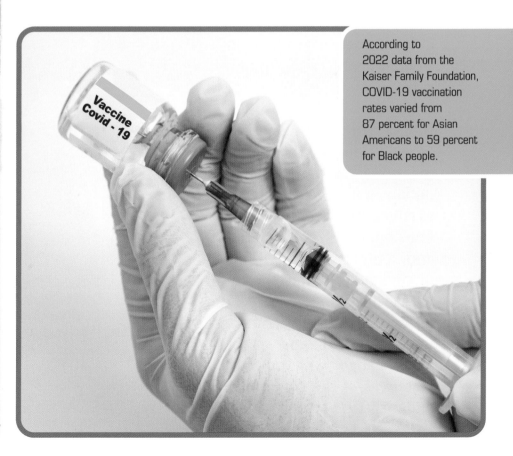

According to 2022 data from the Kaiser Family Foundation, COVID-19 vaccination rates varied from 87 percent for Asian Americans to 59 percent for Black people.

The reasons behind these disparities are complex. Some racial and ethnic groups experience obstacles to health care, such as a lack of access to insurance or medical providers. Factors such as genetics, personal lifestyle decisions, and social and economic circumstances also affect people's health.

Racism is sometimes described as a public health issue. Some cities and counties have taken the step of declaring racial inequality a public health crisis. Framing it in these terms encourages policy makers to address the root causes of disparities. In addition to health care measures, this would include initiatives involving areas such as education, criminal justice, housing, transportation, and employment. Millions of individuals have raised their voices in recent years over the issue of racial injustice. Bringing about real change will take the resources of the government and private sector, as well.

Racial and ethnic minorities are more likely to suffer from severe illness or death from a range of conditions such as diabetes and heart disease.

CHAPTER 4

SURVIVING AND THRIVING

Experiences with racial inequality can make young people feel anxious, angry, sad, and confused. Teens are struggling with their own identities and beginning to assert their independence during high school. Grappling with the injustice of racial inequality during this time can sometimes become overwhelming. Parents may want to protect their children from raw experiences of racism, and teachers may try to approach the issue with sensitivity, but most adolescents can't be shielded from racism in today's digitally connected world.

Unfortunately, it will probably be a long time before any or all forms of racial inequality are wiped out in our society. The best you can do—especially if you are a person of color—is to arm yourself with knowledge and develop the coping skills to keep yourself sane, and to maintain your self-respect and self-esteem. Taking care of yourself is essential, so know what you need to do to keep yourself healthy and strong.

Even teenagers who don't experience racial inequality in their daily lives may witness racist hate and intolerance on social media.

THE TOLL OF MICROAGGRESSIONS

You may not have been the victim of loud, overt racism, but chances are you have experienced what the experts call microaggressions. This term was first used by psychiatrist Dr. Chester Pierce in the 1970s and then later expanded upon by psychologist Dr. Derald Wing Sue at Columbia University. Microaggressions are what is known as unintended discrimination. Dr. Sue defined them as "brief and commonplace daily, verbal, behavioral, or environmental indignities, whether intentional or unintentional, that communicate hostile, derogatory, or negative racial slights and insults towards people of color."

These actions or comments are often subtle and they unintentionally or unconsciously reinforce negative racial stereotypes. Some examples include a white girl tightening her hold on her purse when a Latino person walks nearby, an Asian American being complimented for speaking "such good English," a Black couple being seated near the kitchen in a restaurant even though there are better tables available, or a Native American being told, "Wow, I don't even think of you as an Indian."

It is likely that, most of the time, microaggressions are not meant to be insulting, yet they can certainly feel demeaning under certain circumstances. So, how do you handle them? Recognize that you're not being overly sensitive. Feeling hurt or angry is normal. You might be able to let it go, especially if you really like the person who made the comment. You can just choose to walk away from the moment.

Microggressions can be directed at any marginalized group based on factors such as race, gender, ethnicity, religion, disability, sexual orientation, or gender identity.

Other times, the experience may fester like a wound and that's when you need to take some action. As psychologist Ellen Hendrikson writes online, "Trust yourself. If the comment sticks with you, even hours later, or it makes you mad or sad to replay in your head what happened, know you don't have to swallow it like a hot coal. Tell someone," she continues. "Talk to someone who gets it, no matter their color." Find a friend, parent, relative, teacher, or other trusted adult and explain how you feel.

Another way to respond to microaggressions is to take a minute and ask the person, "What did you mean by that comment?" Often this question is enough to make the person more aware of what he or she has just said. You might also try saying, "That comment was pretty offensive to Hispanics" or "You know, comments like that might be upsetting to Black people." You might even personalize the statement and say, "It hurts my feelings when people say those things, because . . ."

These are fairly gentle ways of teaching an important lesson. Speaking honestly and tactfully is often the key to getting through to others. If you let your frustration guide you, your words may come out angry and that can elicit defensiveness in the other person. If that happens, the lesson will most likely be lost, and a relationship may end.

It is one problem when you are coping with racist behavior from friends or classmates. But what happens if it is coming from a teacher or other faculty member at your school? Current statistics show that about 80 percent of the country's school teachers are white. This can cause racial issues in a number of classrooms.

If you believe a teacher is treating you differently because of your race, be sure to write down all the details you possibly can. Exactly what happened and when? What was said and by whom? Did anyone else witness it? Take this information to your parents or other trusted adult. Ask to see your school's policies on racism. Finally, contact the school administrator and determine who the information should be taken to. With your parents or other adults, present your evidence factually and clearly. Hopefully the school will investigate what is happening and you will either see immediate changes—or a different teacher in the front of the classroom.

Black students are more likely to consider careers in education if they themselves have been motivated by Black teachers in the classroom.

SYSTEMIC RACISM

In his Inaugural Address on January 20, 2021, President Joe Biden mentioned that systemic racism is one of the challenges facing the United States. Systemic racism—sometimes called structural racism or institutional racism—refers to the laws, regulations, policies, and practices that reinforce racial disparities in areas such as the criminal justice system, employment opportunities, income and wealth, housing, environmental justice, health, politics, and education. Systemic racism goes beyond the racist actions and attitudes of individuals or even groups. Systemic racism may be a factor when people of color find it more difficult to find a job, get a loan to buy a house, or send their kids to a good school. Employers, banks, and local school systems don't intentionally discriminate, but hiring practices, lending policies, and school funding systems may put people of color at a disadvantage.

Systemic racism is difficult to address because it's so entrenched. Historically, minorities have had fewer opportunities to build wealth, and disparities in income and wealth continue to leave minority groups behind. The American Bar Association points out some of the racial inequities of the criminal justice system—for example, although Black people make up 14 percent of the U.S. population, they're incarcerated in state prisons at five times the rate of white people. Reducing the harm caused by structural racism will take action by the government, business interests, advocacy groups, and individuals who genuinely believe that all Americans should have equal opportunities.

Systemic racism exists across society and results in racial disparities in areas such as employment, income, housing, health care, and education.

PRACTICING SELF-CARE

Multiple studies have made it clear that ongoing stress is hard on your emotional, mental, and physical health. Keeping your stress levels down is truly important. It will not only make you a calmer and healthier person, but it will make it easier to make the best decisions on how to deal with any racial issues you encounter. How can you help keep your stress levels down?

Good self-care can help you cope with sources of stress in your life, including racial inequality. Self-care refers to practices that promote good physical, mental, and emotional health. Taking time for self-care isn't a luxury or indulgence—you shouldn't think that you're spoiling yourself by reserving time for your basic well-being. Rather, self-care is a positive habit that will help you cope with challenges and overcome obstacles in your daily life. Establishing good self-care practices when you're young will help give you a solid foundation later on for dealing with adult responsibilities and working to achieve your ambitions. Here are a few ideas to try:

Make a conscious effort to practice self-care—even a few small acts every day can benefit both your mental and physical health.

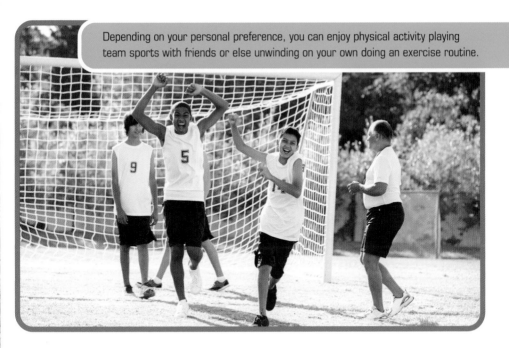

Depending on your personal preference, you can enjoy physical activity playing team sports with friends or else unwinding on your own doing an exercise routine.

Surround yourself with a strong support system of friends and family. These people love you and are typically willing to do whatever you need—from giving you a great big hug to lending an ear when you need to vent.

Join any possible student associations for people of color. Being around like-minded people can make everything easier because they understand exactly what you are going through and often have great advice and suggestions.

Take care of your body. This means doing the things your parents keep telling you to do—get enough sleep at night, exercise, and eat healthy food. Physical activity is a great way to release stress, but do not push yourself to do something you do not enjoy. If you hate running, don't focus on jogging. There are many fun ways to get exercise, including skateboarding, hiking, biking, or swimming.

Spend time doing what you enjoy most. No matter how busy you are, find a way to make time for whatever hobbies you like to do. Being creative is a great way to relax and feel better about yourself and the world.

Read supportive and helpful books and other resources. Check out your local library and see what kind of materials they might have about racial inequality and how to deal with it. Ask if there are any support groups or upcoming programs geared to the topic. (If there aren't, now is the time for you to suggest that changes!) Meditate, get outside, or do some deep breathing. All of these activities will help your body and mind relax.

Meditation can help reduce stress and improve overall well-being, and it's easy to practice almost anywhere or at any time.

If you're feeling overwhelmed or have symptoms such as sleeplessness or trouble concentrating, a mental health professional such as a counselor or therapist can help you work through your issues.

SEEKING HELP AND TAKING ACTION

What happens when you meditate, sleep well, read books, and talk to your friends and it still isn't enough? It might be time to seek out the guidance and help of a professional. You could start with your school's counselor, or you can try to talk to your parents about seeing a certified therapist, psychiatrist, or psychologist. These experts can help you explore your feelings, plus help you find the resources you need to cope with and control your stress levels. Just being able to talk about your experiences is frequently a relief.

In addition to seeing a counselor of some type, you can also call one of the many hotlines available for teens struggling with various issues, including the impact of racial inequality, like Teen Line at 800-852-8336, the National Suicide Prevention Lifeline at 1-800-273-TALK, and the 988 Suicide & Crisis Lifeline.

What if you are not the one dealing directly with racism, but instead see it happening around you and want to effect some type of change? In a speech in Cleveland, Ohio, Margaret Mitchell, president and CEO of YWCA, encouraged everyone to get involved in ending racial inequality. As reported by the Not In Our Town website, she told her audience:

> There is a cure against racism. The deep wounds can be healed but the healing process is intricate, deliberate and will require involvement from those who have previously remained silent. When racism raises its ugly head, silence becomes toxic and our apathy is interpreted as total acceptance. We always have a choice: do nothing and let racism go uncontested and flourish, or do something— act up, rise up, and speak up. We must pick up the armor of righteousness daily in order to slay the evil forces of racism at work against us . . . It will not be easy and it will not always be comfortable for any of us but courage is a game changer. We must each take a step each day to garner support and find our voice as the moral majority.

In order to act up, rise up, and speak up, as Mitchell recommended, people must make changes. As you work to raise awareness of racial inequality, take stock of your own perspective and preconceptions. Everybody has blind spots in their attitudes toward other people. You may consider yourself free of prejudice, but it's easy to make inaccurate assumptions about others who are different from yourself. Keep an open mind and try to learn from people coming from a variety of cultures, backgrounds, and viewpoints. By clarifying your thinking on issues related to racial inequality, you'll be better able to communicate your convictions to others.

Today's young people are passionate about causes, such as ending racial oppression, and savvy about spreading their message to a wider audience on the latest platforms.

CHAPTER 5

STANDING UP AGAINST INEQUALITY

Recognizing racial inequality in all its forms comes first. Responding to it effectively comes second. Coping in healthy ways is third, and then, at last, is translating these experiences into something positive. When responding to inequality leads to empowerment and helping yourself as well as others, you are definitely the winner.

As seen, European colonists arriving in North America stripped Native Americans of their land and brought diseases that decimated their populations. In the 20th century, the authorities suppressed Native American culture and traditions. More recently, however, many Native Americans have reconnected with their heritage, bringing back languages and practices that had formerly been discouraged or even forbidden.

ACTIVISM AT STANDING ROCK

This sense of pride has also spurred activism among young Native Americans. In the fall of 2016 the world was riveted by a showdown in North Dakota that eerily echoed the battles our nation saw more than a century ago. Once again, Native Americans were put into a position of protecting their land, no matter how long it took or what the final cost might be.

The Texas-based Energy Transfer Partners planned to build a 1,172-mile (1,886 km) pipeline to carry 570,000 barrels of oil each day from North Dakota to Illinois. They ran into a big problem, however: Native American tribes objected. The pipeline would run underneath the Missouri River, which provides the main drinking water for the 10,000 people living on the Standing Rock Sioux reservation. The Sioux worried a leak could contaminate their water supplies. In addition, the pipeline would run through a sacred burial ground.

Opposition to the Dakota Access Pipeline began with petitions and action from youth groups before the cause inspired a national movement that drew international attention.

In the beginning, the protests came from the Sioux, but over time, more and more people joined the debate. Members from hundreds of different tribes came to the battle. Thousands of other people traveled to the area to join and support the water protectors, as they are calling themselves, including celebrities Mark Ruffalo and Shailene Woodley. The protestors were closely monitored by the National Guard and police officers, and many people were arrested. The peaceful protest turned rather violent, with officers using pepper spray, rubber bullets, concussion cannons, and police dogs against unarmed protestors. In early December, federal authorities put a stop to all construction of the Dakota Access Pipeline.

When Donald Trump took office as president in 2017, however, he quickly moved to restart the project. The pipeline was completed by June and began operating.

The battle then moved to court. In 2020, the Standing Rock Sioux Tribe won a victory that struck down a federal permit that violated an environmental law. In 2022, the U.S. Supreme Court upheld the lower court ruling. The pipeline will be required to undergo a comprehensive environmental impact statement, representing a major victory for tribes and environmental groups.

RAISING YOUR VOICE

Now that you are more aware of racism and its impact on you, on your life, and on your community and world as a whole, it's time to do something about it. Attending any local support groups is a great step, and organizing a group if one does not exist is terrific. Your involvement does not need to stop there, though.

Protesting against injustice and inequality is important, but demonstrations should be nonviolent. Mohandas Gandhi agreed. "We are constantly being astonished these days at the amazing discoveries in the field of violence," he stated. "But I maintain that far more undreamt of and seemingly impossible discoveries will be made in the field of nonviolence."

Mohandas Gandhi called for strikes, protests, and other means of peaceful resistance to further the cause of Indian independence from Great Britain, inspiring civil rights leaders worldwide.

Peaceful protests are often a wonderful way to bring awareness to issues. They send a strong message but in a way that does not involve anyone getting hurt or feeling threatened. The sit-ins at lunch counters a half century ago are an excellent example. Today's Kaepernick effect is another one. According to the King Center, Martin Luther King Jr. once said, "He who passively accepts evil is as much involved in it as he who helps to perpetuate it. He who accepts evil without protesting against it is really cooperating with it."

Protesting can take many different forms. Sharing your message is always the primary goal. While skywriting or mass petitions might be beyond the scope of your or your group's budget and time, there are many other, smaller projects you can undertake. These include conducting local petitions; picketing or striking; occupying a public space; displaying banners and posters; holding candlelight vigils; singing; walking out; sponsoring sit-ins; encouraging consumer boycotts; making public speeches; writing letters of opposition or support to newspapers and other printed or online media sites; distributing leaflets, pamphlets, and other materials; wearing symbols; and organizing parades or marches.

Organizing protest actions and participating in activism can be a valuable learning experience that helps build your confidence that you can make a difference in the world.

When people come together to work toward a common cause, they can bring attention to injustices and achieve genuine change.

Although peaceful protests are just that—peaceful and nonviolent—always talk to your parents about participating in them first. They may have some advice, input, or precautions they want to share with you. The same may be true for teachers, faculty advisers, guidance counselors, or members of organizations in your area that have experience in these kinds of things.

You may be surprised by the degree of activism in your immediate social circles when you start asking around. There are many people who have and continue to be involved in activism, even if they don't seem like the type to be. Such people can help you learn the ropes, and serve as role models. They may also be able to point you to important works about organizing, including books about people's movements around the world.

You can look up groups online that are active in your city, town, or county. These may be grassroots organizations with only a few people. Think about how energized they might be to unite with your own group. They may even want you to join theirs, or vice versa. The possibilities are endless when you reach out in an earnest, heartfelt manner.

The internet can be a valuable tool in connecting activists and raising awareness about the damage caused by racial inequality.

STAYING SAFE ON SOCIAL MEDIA

We live in a technological environment that the civil rights leaders of the past did not fully anticipate decades ago. The online world is normal and routine to you, but it would be mind-boggling to some of the biggest historical icons of activism. With just a couple clicks or swipes on a keyboard or a screen, you have the ability to share a thought, send a message, post a photo, organize an event, or pose a question to the rest of the world. This makes promoting racial equality concepts, projects, and social movements so much faster. You can post on a social media site, write a blog post, record a podcast, or text a group of friends to gather together in mere minutes.

It is important, however, that you remember to stay safe when utilizing that technology. Protect your identity, as always. Do not reveal too much personal information to the cyber world. There are both internet predators and identity thieves who are more than happy to ignore your cause and take advantage of you.

No matter how you choose to fight racial inequality, your actions make a difference. You can work for change through activism as well as by making an effort to challenge stereotypes and preconceptions about other people in the course of your daily life. Racial inequality doesn't just hurt people from minority groups—it damages American society. Nobody benefits when a segment of the population remains marginalized and vulnerable due in part to circumstances beyond their control. With enough people working together and standing united against racial inequality, you can help achieve real change.

Technology has transformed the ways people share information and raise awareness, but make an effort to maintain civility and protect your privacy when using social media and other online tools.

10 GREAT QUESTIONS TO ASK A COUNSELOR

1. How can I respond to racial insults or treatment?

2. How can I talk to my peers or family if they are clearly racist in their behavior?

3. What are the mental health consequences of discrimination or racism?

4. What self-care approaches can help me deal with stresses caused by racial inequality?

5. Where can I turn if I'm feeling overwhelmed by the hate and pain caused by racial inequality?

6. Where can I find resources that examine the issue of racial inequality?

7. How can I be an ally to marginalized groups?

8. How can I use social media safely and effectively to speak out against racial inequality?

9. What is my community doing to address institutional racism?

10. Are there any organizations in my school or community working to fight racial oppression?

A counselor can help you develop skills to cope with difficult experiences and emotions, such as mental health issues caused by exposure to racism.

advocate: A person who argues for or supports a cause or policy.

assassination: The murder of a political leader or other public figure, usually to make a political point.

bias: Prejudice; a position (well-supported or not) in favor of or against something.

chronic: Continuing or occurring again and again.

civil disobedience: Nonviolent protest used to challenge unfair laws or to voice other political discontent.

discrimination: Unfair treatment based on factors such as a person's race, age, religion, or gender.

diversity: The condition of having many different kinds of people in one's country, community, or establishment.

doctrine: Ideas that are taught as truth.

ethnic: Belonging to a certain group of people who have a culture that is different from the main culture of a country.

harassment: The act of creating a hostile or unpleasant situation for someone through unwanted contact.

icon: A person or thing considered a symbol of something; for example, Martin Luther King Jr. is an icon of the civil rights movement.

indigenous: Having started in and coming naturally from a certain area.

internment camps: Prison camps for confinement of political prisoners or prisoners of war.

microaggression: An unintentional or intentional slight that subtly says something about another's opinion on race or identity that is less hurtful than blatant racism, but may sting nonetheless.

nonviolence: A philosophy of protest and social change in which the participants pledge not to meet the violence of the state or authorities with violence of their own.

oppression: The act of exercising cruel or unjust authority or power over people, including a specific subgroup of people like a religious minority or ethnicity, usually committed by a more powerful group, or the state itself.

peer: A person of the same age, social group, or rank or class as another.

POC: Short for person of color, or people of color, a term used as shorthand when dealing with issues of identity, discrimination, and diversity.

segregated: Set apart or separated from others, especially because of race.

unconscious: Not planned or perceived with full awareness or intention.

AMERICAN CIVIL LIBERTIES UNION

125 Broad Street, 18th Floor
New York, NY 10004
(212) 549-2500
Website: *aclu.org*
Facebook, Twitter: *@ACLU*
Instagram: *@aclu_nationwide*
The ACLU is a nonprofit organization dedicated to protecting and preserving individual liberties and rights guaranteed by the United States Constitution through lobbying and litigation.

CANADIAN CIVIL LIBERTIES ASSOCIATION

400-124 Merton Street
Toronto, ON M4S 2Z2
Canada
(416) 363-0321
Website: *ccla.org*
Facebook, Instagram, Twitter: *@cancivlib*
The Canadian Civil Liberties Association works to educate members of the public about their rights and freedoms and to achieve equality for people throughout Canada.

CENTER FOR CONSTITUTIONAL RIGHTS (CCR)

666 Broadway 7th Floor
New York, NY 10012
(212) 614-6464
ccrjustice.org
Facebook, Instagram: *@CenterforConstitutional-Rights*
Twitter: *@theCCR*
The Center for Constitutional Rights works to fight racial injustice by challenging discriminatory laws and advocating for marginalized communities.

LEADERSHIP CONFERENCE ON CIVIL AND HUMAN RIGHTS

1620 L Street NW Suite 1100
Washington, D.C. 20036
(202) 466-3311
Website: *civilrights.org*
Facebook: *@civilandhumanrights*
Instagram, Twitter: *@civilrightsorg*
The Leadership Conference on Civil and Human Rights unites more than 200 different organizations of different sizes in the United States to work together toward equality for all.

NATIONAL ASSOCIATION FOR THE ADVANCEMENT OF COLORED PEOPLE (NAACP)

4805 Mount Hope Drive
Baltimore, MD 21215
(410) 580-5777
Website: *naacp.org*
Facebook, Instagram, Twitter: *@NAACP*
As one of the oldest civil rights organizations in the United States, the NAACP is a longtime leader in efforts to achieve civic engagement, racial equality, and supportive institutions and policies for people of color.

PSYCHOLOGY TODAY

115 East Twenty-Third Street, Ninth Floor
New York, NY 10010
Website: *www.psychologytoday.com*
Facebook: *@psychologytoday*
Instagram: *@psych_today*
Twitter: *@psychtoday*
Psychology Today is a magazine and online site focusing on psychology and mental health. It provides listings for mental health professionals as well as resources on issues such as dealing with anxiety or depression that can result as the toll of racism.

TEEN LINE

Cedars-Sinai
PO Box 48750
Los Angeles, CA 90048
(800) 852-8336
Email: *admin@teenlineonline.org*
Website: *www.teenline.org*
Facebook, Instagram, Twitter: *@teenlineonline*
The Teen Line helpline offers mental health support provided by trained teen counselors.

Boone, Mary. *Racial Injustice*. San Diego, CA: BrightPoint, 2023.

Davidson, Danica. *Everything You Need to Know About Hate Crimes*. New York, NY: Rosen Publishing, 2018.

Diggs, Barbara. *Race Relations: The Struggle for Equality in America*. White River Junction, VT: Nomad Press, 2019.

Haynes, Danielle. *Racial Profiling and Discrimination*. Buffalo, NY: Rosen Publishing, 2021.

Hinton, Kerry. *Sit-Ins and Nonviolent Protest for Racial Equality*. New York, NY: Rosen Publishing, 2018.

Hurt, Avery Elizabeth. *The Fight for Civil Rights*. New York, NY: Rosen Publishing, 2020.

Jewell, Tiffany. *This Book Is Anti-Racist: 20 Lessons on How to Wake Up, Take Action, and Do the Work*. Minneapolis, MN: Frances Lincoln Children's Books, 2020.

Marcovitz, Hal. *Racial Injustice: Rage, Protests, and Demands for Change.* San Diego, CA: ReferencePoint Press, Inc., 2021.

McGhee, Heather. *The Sum of Us: How Racism Hurts Everyone: Adapted for Young Readers.* New York, NY: Delacorte Press, 2023.

Lo Bosco, Maryellen. *Confronting Racism.* New York, NY: Rosen Publishing, 2018.

Robi, Jill. *Coping with Hate Crimes.* New York, NY: Rosen Publishing, 2019.

Scientific American Editors. *Confronting Racism.* Buffalo, NY: Rosen Publishing, 2023.

Saidian, Siyavush. *Did the Civil Rights Movement Achieve Civil Rights?* New York, NY: Rosen Publishing, 2019.

Timmons, Angie. *Everything You Need to Know About Racism.* New York, NY: Rosen Publishing, 2018.

A

B

C

D

ROBIN BAUSER has written numerous books for children and young adults, including titles addressing current events issues affecting teens. Bauser lives in Chicago.

PHOTO CREDITS